JACKET POTATO FILLINGS

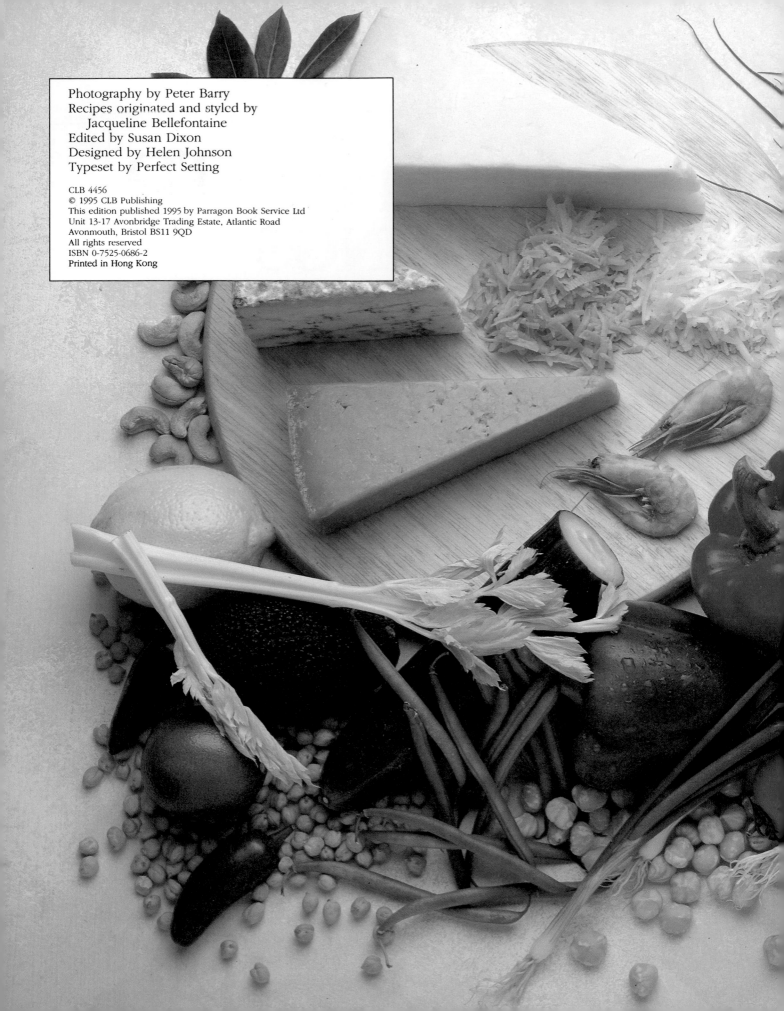

Photography by Peter Barry
Recipes originated and styled by
   Jacqueline Bellefontaine
Edited by Susan Dixon
Designed by Helen Johnson
Typeset by Perfect Setting

CLB 4456
© 1995 CLB Publishing
This edition published 1995 by Parragon Book Service Ltd
Unit 13-17 Avonbridge Trading Estate, Atlantic Road
Avonmouth, Bristol BS11 9QD
All rights reserved
ISBN 0-7525-0686-2
Printed in Hong Kong

JACKET POTATO FILLINGS

||| •PARRAGON• |||

Contents

Introduction

The jacket potato, everyone's favourite! Be it for a light snack, an accompaniment to another dish or as a substantial meal in itself, the jacket potato is a favourite choice. This is not surprising as there can be few more versatile vegetables than the potato. Baked in their jackets with cheese and butter or with olive oil and herbs, potatoes are an easy, inexpensive and absolutely delicious dish. But you need not stop there. The potato itself has a subtle flavour which makes it a perfect foil for many other flavours and textures.

You will find this book packed full of ideas, with something for everyone. There are not only low calorie fillings such as the slimmer's delight, and crunchy chicken and sweetcorn topping, to suit the weight conscious, but also hearty and substantial fillings which include chilli, Potatoes with Monkfish Creole and Special Baked Beans, all of which make ideal main meals for all the family. You'll also find quick and simple fillings that turn a plain jacket potato into a real treat; fillings that the kids will love, as well as a selection just right for one or two people. There are even some for special occasions.

The Perfect Jacket Potato
Before you start to choose the filling, you need to know how to cook the perfect potato. Choose potatoes of even size, about 275g/10oz each is just right.

To cook the Potatoes:
1. Preheat the oven to 200°C/400°F/Gas mark 6.
2. Scrub unwashed potatoes thoroughly and prick all over with a fork. This will prevent the potato from bursting during cooking. Brush with a little melted butter or sunflower oil if desired.
3. Place on a baking tray and bake for 1 to 1¼ hours or until soft when gently squeezed.
4. Serve lightly seasoned with a knob of butter or with a filling of your choice.

You do not need any special equipment to bake potatoes, but you can reduce the cooking time slightly (about 10 to 15 minutes) if you push a metal skewer through the centre of each potato or use a special potato roaster which has four metal spikes on which to place the potatoes. Both these methods allow heat to be conducted to the centre of the potato, thus decreasing the cooking time.

Microwave Jacket Potatoes
Using a microwave to cook potatoes cuts down on the cooking time dramatically, but unfortunately you do not get the lovely crispy skin you get when you bake them in a conventional oven. Nonetheless microwaves can be jolly handy if you are cooking just one or two potatoes, or when you simply need a meal in double quick time. Most of the fillings in

this book can be used in a microwave although a few are not suitable and these are indicated in the cook's tips. As it only requires a little extra effort to turn on the oven and the end results are better, if you have the time it will be well worth the wait.

To microwave Jacket Potatoes:

Scrub and prick the potatoes with a fork. Do NOT brush with oil or butter. Arrange in the microwave in a circle on a piece of absorbent kitchen paper. Microwave on 100 per cent (High) for the required time, turning over halfway through the cooking.

One potato will take about 4 to 6 minutes, two will take about 10 to 12 minutes and four about 18 to 20 minutes.

These timings are based on using 275g/10oz potatoes in a 650W microwave oven. For different sized potatoes and different wattage ovens you will need to adjust the timings accordingly.

Buying and Storing Potatoes

Buy the freshest samples available. They should be free of damage and clean, with smooth, tight skins. Avoid potatoes that have wrinkly skins, green patches or that are beginning to sprout. Store in a cool, dark place. You can buy ready cleaned and graded potatoes just for baking, but remember, washed potatoes will not last as long as the unwashed variety and are best used on the day of purchase.

Potato Varieties

Although almost any large potatoes can be used for baking, different varieties give different results. Some have fluffier textured flesh, others produce a crisper skin and have a slightly sweet flavour, so it is well worth trying different varieties to find your favourite. The best potatoes for baking include Cara, Desiree, King Edward, Maris Piper and Romano. Other suitable varieties include Estima, Marfona, Pentland Dell, Pentland Squire and Wilja.

Potatoes for a Healthy Diet

With the greater awareness of healthy eating the nutritional value of the potato should be appreciated. Current medical advice suggests we should be eating more unrefined starchy foods like pasta, rice and, of course, potatoes (though not fried!). Potatoes contain valuable vitamins and minerals such as vitamin C, Vitamin B6, Calcium and Copper and they are also a good source of fibre particularly if the skins are eaten.

With 52 tempting fillings to choose from, you can easily include jacket potatoes as a regular part of a healthy diet. One thing is certain: you will never get bored with the humble spud, so go on, make a meal of jacket potatoes.

CHICKEN AND APRICOT CURRY

Spicy curries go as well with potatoes as they do with
their traditional accompaniment – rice.

SERVES 4

4 large baking potatoes
4 chicken breasts, skinned, boned and cut
    into bite-size pieces
½ tsp chilli powder
2 tsp garam masala
2.5 cm/1 inch piece root ginger, peeled and
    grated
2 cloves garlic, crushed
2 tbsps ghee or sunflower oil
1 tbsp curry paste
1 large onion, cut into wedges
400g/14oz can chopped tomatoes
60g/2oz no-soak dried apricots, chopped
1 tsp sugar
4 tsps white wine vinegar
Salt

1. Cook the potatoes as directed (see Introduction).

2. Put the chicken in a bowl.

3. Mix together the chilli powder, garam masala, ginger and garlic. Sprinkle this over the chicken, and toss to coat well.

4. Allow the chicken to stand for 1-2 hours fully to absorb the flavours.

5. Melt the ghee or heat the oil in a large frying pan and add the spiced chicken and the curry paste.

6. Toss over a high heat for 5 minutes until the chicken is browned.

Remove from the pan and set aside.

7. Add the onion along with a little more ghee or oil if necessary, and fry for 5 minutes until just softened.

8. Return the chicken to the pan and add the tomatoes and apricots. Cook for 20 minutes.

9. Stir in the sugar and vinegar, and cook for a further 10 minutes.

10. Cut in half and top with the curry

TIME: Preparation takes about 15 minutes plus 2 hours standing.
Cooking takes approximately 40 minutes.

VARIATION: Diced turkey can be used in this recipe in place of the chicken.

COOK'S TIP: This dish is delicious served with a tomato and onion salad.

POTATOES WITH SWEET AND SOUR PORK

A Chinese influence is given to this tasty potato dish.

SERVES 4

---

4 large baking potatoes
340g/12oz lean pork, cubed
2 tbsps cornflour
4 tbsps sunflower oil
1 onion, sliced
1 tbsp tomato purée
1 clove garlic, crushed
1 tbsp soy sauce
2 tbsps white wine vinegar
2 tbsps clear honey
1 tbsp dry sherry
280 ml/½ pint chicken stock
2.5 cm/1 inch piece root ginger grated
½ green pepper, seeded and sliced
½ red pepper, seeded and sliced

---

1. Cook the potatoes as directed (see Introduction).

2. Toss the meat in the cornflour.

3. Heat half the oil in a large frying pan and fry the onion until softened. Remove with a draining spoon and set aside.

4. Add the remaining oil and fry the meat for 5 minutes or until browned on all sides.

5. Return the onion to the pan.

6. Stir in the remaining ingredients and bring gently to the boil.

7. Reduce the heat and simmer gently for 30-35 minutes or until the meat is tender.

8. When the potatoes are cooked, cut in half and mash the flesh slightly if liked. Spoon over the pork mixture and serve immediately.

TIME: Preparation takes about 10 minutes. Cooking takes approximately 45 minutes.

BROAD BEAN AND BACON STUFFED POTATOES

Broad beans and bacon make a delicious combination.

SERVES 4

4 large baking potatoes
2 tbsp sunflower oil
1 onion, chopped
1 clove garlic, crushed
120g/4oz diced bacon (smoked if possible)
175g/6oz frozen broad beans
Salt and pepper
1 tbsp chopped fresh mixed herbs or 1 tsp
    dried mixed herbs
60g/2oz Cheddar cheese, grated
2 tbsps grated Parmesan cheese
Fresh herbs to garnish

1. Cook the potatoes as directed (see Introduction).

2. Heat the oil in a frying pan and fry the onion for 3-4 minutes or until beginning to soften.

3. Add the garlic and fry gently for 1 minute.

4. Increase the heat and add the bacon, then fry for about 5 minutes or until beginning to crisp.

5. Cook the beans in boiling water for 3-4 minutes, drain well and add to the pan. Stir in the salt, pepper and herbs.

6. When the potatoes are cooked, cut in half and scoop out the flesh. Mash well.

7. Beat the beans and bacon into the potato and pile back into the potato skins

8. Mix together the two cheeses and sprinkle over the potatoes. Brown under a preheated grill and serve immediately. Garnish with mixed herbs.

TIME: Preparation takes about 10 minutes. Cooking takes approximately 15 minutes.

SERVING IDEAS: Serve as a light meal or as an accompaniment to other dishes.

HAM AND BROCCOLI STUFFED POTATOES

A great supper dish for all the family.

SERVES 4

---

4 large baking potatoes
225g/8oz broccoli florets
30g/1oz butter
30g/1oz plain flour
280ml/½ pint milk
Salt and pepper
Pinch of grated nutmeg
60g/2oz sweetcorn kernels
175g/6oz ham, diced

---

1. Cook the potatoes as directed (see Introduction).

2. Cook the broccoli in lightly salted boiling water for 5 minutes. Drain well.

3. Melt the butter in a saucepan. Stir in the flour and cook over a low heat for 1 minute.

4. Remove from the heat and gradually add the milk, stirring well after each addition.

5. Return the pan to the heat and cook over a low heat until thickened, stirring constantly.

6. Season to taste with salt, pepper and nutmeg.

7. Add the cooked broccoli, the sweetcorn and ham, and heat through.

8. When the potatoes are cooked, cut in half and scoop out the flesh. Mash well.

9. Add the broccoli and ham mixture and beat until well combined.

10. Spoon back into the potato skins and serve.

TIME: Preparation takes about 5 minutes. Cooking takes approximately 10 minutes.

WATCHPOINT: Take care not to overcook the broccoli at the beginning or it will disintegrate completely.

THAI STYLE CHICKEN

Coconut milk is used in this Thai-influenced curry.
It gives the curry a wonderfully mild and creamy flavour.

SERVES 4

4 large baking potatoes
2 tbsps sunflower oil
1 onion, chopped
4 chicken breasts, skinned, boned and cut
 into bite-size cubes
2 cloves garlic, crushed
1 tbsp Thai red curry paste
200ml/7 fl oz can coconut milk
1 tbsp sugar
Grated zest and juice of ½ lime
1 tsp light soy sauce
1 tbsp chopped fresh coriander
Sprigs coriander to garnish

1. Cook the potatoes as directed (see Introduction).

2. Heat the oil in a wok or large frying pan and fry the onion and chicken for 5 minutes until softened and beginning to brown.

3. Stir in the garlic and cook for 2 minutes. Remove the onion, chicken and garlic with a slotted spoon and set aside.

4. Add the curry paste and cook for 1-2 minutes, then stir in half the coconut milk and boil rapidly for 3 minutes.

5. Return the chicken to the wok, then stir in the sugar, lime zest, juice and soy sauce. Simmer gently for 5 minutes or until the chicken is cooked through.

6. Stir in the remaining coconut milk and the chopped coriander, and cook until heated through.

7. When the potatoes are cooked, cut in half and mash flesh if desired. Spoon over the curry and serve immediately, garnished with sprigs of coriander.

TIME: Preparation takes about 15 minutes. Cooking takes approximately 15 minutes.

VARIATION: For a hotter, spicier curry use Thai green curry paste instead of red curry paste.

WATCH POINT: Remember to shake the can well before measuring the coconut milk.

LIVER PATÉ AND ORANGE STUFFED POTATOES

This unusual filling can be knocked up in minutes.

SERVES 4

4 medium baking potatoes
175g/6oz smooth liver paté
60g/2oz cream cheese
2 tbsps natural yogurt
Salt and pepper
Grated zest of ½ orange
2 tbsps orange juice
Orange segments and gherkin fans, to
    garnish

1. Cook the potatoes as directed (see Introduction).

2. Cut the tops off the potatoes and scoop the flesh into a bowl. Mash well.

3. In a medium sized bowl, beat the pâté until slightly softened, then beat in the cream cheese followed by the natural yogurt.

4. Beat the pâté mixture into the potato flesh, then season to taste with salt and pepper.

5. Stir in the orange zest and juice and pile the mixture back into the potato skins, or spoon into a piping bag and pipe the mixture into the potatoes.

6. Return to the oven for 10-15 minutes to heat through and serve garnished with orange segments and gherkin fans.

TIME: Preparation takes about 10 minutes. Reheating takes approximately 15 minutes.

VARIATION: Ring the changes by using a different smooth pâté to make this dish.

SERVING IDEAS: Halve the quantity and use smaller potatoes to make this an unusual starter.

MICROWAVE NOTES: If cooking the potatoes in a microwave, reheat for 2-3 minutes on 100% (high).

SIMPLE SAVOURY MINCE FILLING

A savoury mince filling goes perfectly with baked potatoes.
Add a simple salad garnish and the meal is complete.

SERVES 4

4 large baking potatoes
2 tbsps sunflower oil
1 large onion, chopped
1 clove garlic, crushed
340g/12oz lean minced pork
1 green pepper, seeded and chopped
120g/4oz mushrooms, sliced
400g/14oz can chopped tomatoes with
    herbs
2 tbsps tomato purée

1. Cook the potatoes as directed (see Introduction).

2. Heat the oil in a frying pan and fry the onion until just beginning to soften.

3. Add the garlic and fry for a further minute.

4. Add the minced pork and fry until brown.

5. Stir in the pepper, mushrooms, tomatoes and tomato purée. Bring to the boil, then reduce the heat and simmer gently for 30 minutes.

6. When the potatoes are cooked, cut a wedge out of the top of each one. Scoop out the flesh and mash if liked. Return to the skins.

7. Spoon the mince on top and serve.

TIME: Preparation takes about 10 minutes. Cooking takes approximately 40 minutes.

VARIATION: Use lamb or beef mince if desired.

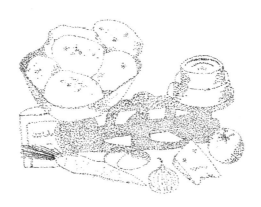

MINI SATÉ AND PEANUT SAUCE

The potatoes are topped with beef kebabs and an aromatic sauce.

SERVES 4

4 large baking potatoes
225g/8oz fillet or sirloin steak, cut into small
 cubes
Grated zest and juice of ½ lime
3 tbsps sunflower oil
½ tsp crushed dried chillies
Pinch of turmeric
Pinch of cumin
1 small onion, chopped
¼ tsp chilli powder
6 tbsps water
6 tbsps peanut butter
Salt and pepper
Fresh coriander, to garnish

1. Cook the potatoes as directed (see Introduction).

2. Thread the steak onto 8 cocktail sticks. Place in a shallow dish.

3. Mix together the lime zest, juice, 2 tbsps of the oil, the crushed chillies, turmeric and cumin. Pour this over the meat.

4. Allow the meat to marinate for 30 minutes, turning occasionally.

5. Heat the remaining oil in a small saucepan and fry the onion until soft.

6. Add the chilli powder and fry for 1 minute, then stir in the water and peanut butter. Simmer gently for 5 minutes, stirring occasionally.

7. Cook the kebabs under a preheated grill for 5-10 minutes, turning once.

8. When the potatoes are cooked, cut the tops off each one and scoop the flesh into a bowl. Mash well. Season with salt and pepper and pile back into the potato skins. Spoon the peanut sauce on top and sprinkle with a little chopped fresh coriander. Serve with the kebabs and garnish with a sprig of coriander.

TIME: Preparation takes about 10 minutes plus 30 minutes marinating. Cooking takes approximately 15 minutes.

VARIATION: Use skinned and boned chicken breasts in place of the steak.

23

EASY CHILLI FILLING

This version of a very popular filling for potatoes is simple to prepare.

SERVES 4

---

4 large baking potatoes
1 tbsp sunflower oil
1 small onion, chopped
340g/12oz lean minced beef
1 tsp chilli powder
140ml/¼ pint beef stock
200g/7oz can red kidney beans, drained and
  rinsed
4 tomatoes, skinned if liked and roughly
  chopped
1 tbsp tomato purée

1. Cook the potatoes as directed (see Introduction).

2. Heat the oil in a saucepan and fry the onion until soft. Add the minced beef and continue to cook until browned.

3. Stir in the chilli powder and cook for 1 minute.

4. Stir the stock, beans, tomatoes and tomato purée into the pan and bring gently to the boil.

5. Reduce the heat and simmer for 20 minutes or until the meat is tender.

6. When the potatoes are cooked, cut the top off each one and mash the flesh if liked. Pour the chilli over the top and serve.

TIME: Preparation takes about 5 minutes. Cooking takes approximately 30 minutes.

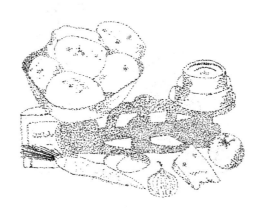

SPICY TOMATO AND CHORIZO TOPPING

A combination from the Mediterranean of spicy sausage and fresh tomatoes.
Use plum tomatoes if you can get them as these give the best flavour.

SERVES 4

4 large baking potatoes
2 tbsps olive oil
1 Spanish onion, chopped
3 cloves garlic, crushed
1 tsp paprika
450g/1lb tomatoes, preferably plum, skinned (optional) and roughly chopped
4 sun-dried tomato halves in olive oil, sliced
150g/5oz chorizo or other spicy sausage, sliced

1. Cook the potatoes as directed (see Introduction).

2. Heat the oil in a saucepan and fry the onion until soft and beginning to brown.

3. Add the garlic and paprika and fry for a further 2 minutes.

4. Stir in the chopped tomatoes and sun-dried tomatoes. Bring gently to the boil.

5. Add the chorizo to the pan. Reduce the heat and simmer gently for 20-25 minutes.

6. When the potatoes are cooked cut a cross in the top of each one. Using a tea-towel, gently squeeze each potato to open out the cross slightly. Pile the sausage mixture on top and serve.

TIME: Preparation takes about 10 minutes. Cooking takes approximately 30 minutes.

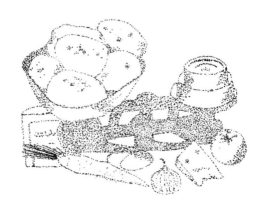

SHERRIED LIVER WITH MUSHROOMS

Both mouth-watering and nutritious and easy to make.

SERVES 4

---

4 large baking potatoes
2 tbsps sunflower oil
1 onion, chopped
2 cloves garlic, crushed
225g/8oz mushrooms, sliced
225g/8oz veal liver, cut into strips
4 tbsps sherry

---

1. Cook the potatoes as directed (see Introduction).

2. Heat the oil in a frying pan and fry the onion and garlic until beginning to soften.

3. Stir in the mushrooms and fry for 3-4 minutes or until soft. Remove from the pan and keep warm.

4. Add the liver and cook over a low heat for 5 minutes or until cooked through.

5. Remove with a slotted spoon and add to the mushrooms.

6. Pour any juices that have come from the mushrooms into the pan, then, with the pan away from the heat, add the sherry and stir well.

7. Return to the heat and bring to the boil. Simmer for 2 minutes.

8. When the potatoes are cooked. Slice the top off each one and scoop out the flesh. Pour over the juices from the pan and mash well.

9. Pile back into the skins and serve with the liver and mushrooms.

TIME: Preparation takes about 10 minutes. Cooking takes approximately 15 minutes.

WATCHPOINT: Do not overcook the liver as it will become very tough.

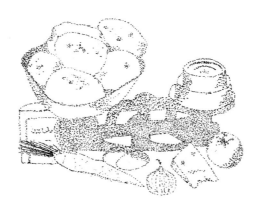

CREAMY BACON AND MUSHROOM TOPPING

Use plain or smoked bacon according to taste.

SERVES 4

4 large baking potatoes
6 rashers back bacon
60g/2oz butter
2 cloves garlic, crushed
6 spring onions, sliced
225g/8oz mushrooms, sliced
1 tsp cornflour
A little milk
Pinch of grated nutmeg
200g/7oz tub creamy fromage frais (8% fat)
Salt and pepper

1. Cook the potatoes as directed (see Introduction).

2. Remove the rind from the bacon and discard. Cut the bacon into strips.

3. Melt the butter in a frying pan and sauté the bacon and garlic until the bacon begins to brown. Stir in the spring onions and mushrooms and sauté for 5-6 minutes or until the mushrooms are soft.

4. Mix the cornflour to a smooth paste with a little milk, then stir into the pan. Add the nutmeg, then stir in the fromage frais. Bring carefully to simmering point and simmer for 2 minutes, trying not to let the mixture boil. Season to taste with salt, pepper and nutmeg.

5. When the potatoes are cooked, cut a cross in the top of each one. Using a tea-towel, gently squeeze each potato to open out the cross slightly.

6. Spoon the mushroom mixture on top and serve immediately.

TIME: Preparation takes about 15 minutes. Cooking takes approximately 10 minutes.

WATCHPOINT: Do not use the very low-fat fromage frais in this recipe as it will curdle.

SAUSAGE, EGG AND BACON JACKETS

This traditional and popular combination is an unusual way of serving potatoes.

SERVES 4

4 large baking potatoes
6 pork chipolatas
6 rashers streaky bacon
30g/1oz butter
4 tsps brown fruity sauce
2 hard-boiled eggs, roughly chopped

1. Cook the potatoes as directed (see Introduction).

2. Cut the chipolatas in half to form smaller sausages.

3. Remove the rind from the bacon and discard. Stretch the bacon with the back of a knife and cut into two pieces.

4. Wrap each sausage in a piece of bacon and thread 3 sausages on one cocktail stick, to make 4 mini kebabs.

5. Place on a baking sheet and cook alongside the potatoes for 25 minutes, or cook under a preheated grill.

6. Cut the tops off the cooked potatoes and scoop the flesh into a bowl. Mash well with the butter and fruity sauce.

7. Stir in the chopped egg. Spoon back into the potato skins and return to the oven for 10 minutes.

8. Top the potatoes with the sausage kebabs and serve with baked beans.

TIME: Preparation takes about 10 minutes.
Cooking takes approximately 10 minutes, plus reheating.

MICROWAVE NOTES: If cooking the potatoes in a microwave,
reheat for 2-3 minutes on 100% (high).

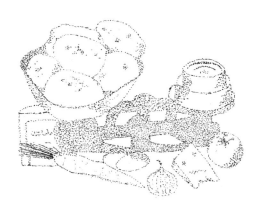

CORNED BEEF HASH

A handy store cupboard standby, corned beef can easily be mixed with just a few other ingredients to make a tempting filling.

SERVES 4

4 large baking potatoes
2 tbsps sunflower oil
1 small onion, chopped
340g/12oz can corned beef, cubed
Salt and pepper
1 tsp mixed dried herbs
60ml/4 tbsps tomato sauce

1. Cook the potatoes as directed (see Introduction).

2. Heat the oil in a large frying pan and fry the onion until soft and beginning to turn golden.

3. Add the corned beef and cook for a further 2 minutes.

4. Season with salt and pepper and stir in the herbs and tomato sauce, mixing well.

5. When the potatoes are cooked, cut in half, scoop out the flesh and roughly cut into cubes.

6. Add to the corned beef and mix together, taking care not to break up the corned beef too much.

7. Heat gently, then pile back into the potato skins and serve.

Time: Preparation takes about 10 minutes. Cooking takes approximately 15 minutes.

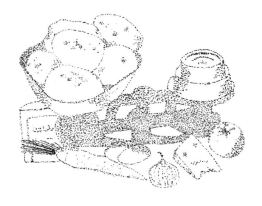

POTATOES WITH PAN FRIED GOULASH

This meat dish with its Hungarian origins is quick to prepare and cook. Use a tender cut of beef.

SERVES 4

4 large baking potatoes
2 tbsps sunflower oil
1 onion, sliced
1 clove garlic, crushed
225g/8oz fillet or sirloin steak, cut into thin
    strips
2 tsps paprika
1 tbsp plain flour
Salt and pepper
200g/7oz can chopped tomatoes
1 tbsp tomato purée
2 tbsps fresh soured cream
Watercress and paprika, to garnish

1. Cook the potatoes as directed (see Introduction).

2. Heat the oil in a frying pan and fry the onion until beginning to soften. Stir in the garlic and fry for 1 minute.

3. Add the meat and toss over the heat until browned on all sides.

4. Stir in the paprika, flour and seasoning and fry for 1 minute, stirring constantly to prevent burning.

5. Stir in the tomatoes and tomato purée and bring gently to the boil. Simmer for 5 minutes.

6. When the potatoes are cooked, cut the tops off each one and mash the flesh if liked.

7. Top with the goulash and soured cream. Garnish with watercress and a sprinkling of paprika on top of the cream.

TIME: Preparation takes about 10 minutes. Cooking takes approximately 10 minutes.

BUBBLE AND SQUEAK JACKETS

*This is a great dish for using up leftover cabbage
or to encourage youngsters to eat their greens.*

SERVES 4

4 large baking potatoes
30g/1oz butter
1 onion, chopped
340g/12oz cooked cabbage, chopped
2-3 slices corned beef, cut into pieces
Salt and pepper

1. Cook the potatoes as directed (see Introduction).

2. Melt the butter in a frying pan and fry the onion over a low heat until soft.

3. Add the cabbage and toss over the heat for 2-3 minutes or until heated through.

4. Add the corned beef to the pan, and cook for 1 minute.

5. Cut the cooked potatoes in half and scoop the flesh into a bowl. Mash well and add to the pan. Season to taste and mix until well combined.

6. Cook over a low heat for 10 minutes, stirring frequently to prevent the potato from burning on the base of the pan.

7. Pile back into the potato skins and serve.

TIME: Preparation takes about 5 minutes. Cooking takes approximately 20 minutes.

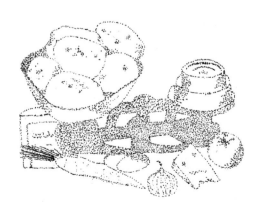

SMOKED COD AND BROCCOLI FILLING

Very suitable as a supper dish. Alternatively, reduce the filling
by half and serve in small potatoes for an unusual starter.

SERVES 4

4 large baking potatoes
225g/8oz smoked cod, skinned
140ml/¼ pint milk
Salt and pepper
Pinch of grated nutmeg
120g/4oz broccoli florets
30g/1oz butter
30g/1oz plain flour
Oil

1. Bake the potatoes as directed (see Introduction).

2. Put the cod in an ovenproof dish. Pour over the milk. Season with salt, pepper, and nutmeg.

3. Cover with foil and cook alongside the potatoes for 20 minutes.

4. When the fish is cooked, drain off the liquid and make up to 280ml/½ pint with water, then set aside. Flake the fish and set aside.

5. Cook the broccoli florets in lightly salted boiling water for 5 minutes. Drain well, and set aside.

6. Melt the butter in a saucepan. Stir in the flour and cook over a low heat for 1 minute.

7. Remove from the heat and gradually add the reserved cooking liquid, stirring well after each addition.

8. Return the pan to the heat and cook over a low heat until thickened, stirring constantly.

9. Stir in the fish and broccoli.

10. Cut the cooked potatoes in half and scoop out the flesh. Mash well, then spoon into a piping bag.

11. Spoon the fish mixture into half of the potato skins and pipe the potato on top. Discard the remaining potato skins. Brush with a little oil and return to the oven for about 15 minutes to brown tops. Alternatively, brown under a preheated grill and serve immediately.

TIME: Preparation takes about 20 minutes. Cooking takes approximately 30 minutes plus reheating.

VARIATION: Use plain cod or a mixture of the two.

MICROWAVE NOTES: This recipe is not suitable for cooking in a microwave.

SALMON WITH CREAMY DILL SAUCE

*This upmarket topping for potatoes makes a
simple special lunch or supper.*

SERVES 4

4 large baking potatoes
30g/1oz butter
340g/12oz salmon fillet
4 tbsps dry white wine
1 tbsp chopped fresh dill
6 tbsps crème fraîche
Fresh dill and lemon twists, to garnish

1. Cook the potatoes as directed (see Introduction).

2. Melt the butter in a frying pan and cook the fish for 3-4 minutes each side.

3. Remove from the pan and flake the fish, discarding any skin and bones.

4. Add the wine to the pan and bring to the boil. Boil for 1 minute.

5. Stir in the dill and crème fraîche and boil for 2-3 minutes until slightly thickened.

6. Add the fish and heat through.

7. When the potatoes are cooked, cut a cross in the top of each one. Using a tea-towel, gently squeeze each potato to open out the cross slightly.

8. Spoon the salmon on top and serve garnished with sprigs of dill and lemon twists.

TIME: Preparation takes about 5 minutes. Cooking time approximately 12 minutes.

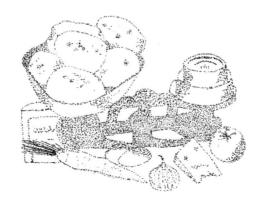

TUNA MAYO TOPPING

The addition of tarragon gives this dish a lovely summery flavour.

SERVES 4

4 large baking potatoes
200g/7oz can tuna chunks, drained
4 spring onions, sliced
½ small red pepper, seeded and finely
 chopped
4 tbsps sweetcorn kernels
1 tsp chopped fresh tarragon or ½ tsp dried
 tarragon
Grated zest of ½ lemon
1 tbsp lemon juice
8 tbsps mayonnaise

1. Cook the potatoes as directed (see Introduction).

2. Place the tuna in a mixing bowl, add the spring onions, red pepper and sweetcorn, and stir until well combined.

3. Mix together the tarragon, lemon zest, juice and mayonnaise, then pour over tuna and mix well.

4. When the potatoes are cooked, cut a cross in the top of each one. Using a tea-towel, gently squeeze each potato to open out the cross slightly.

5. Spoon the tuna mixture on top.

TIME: Preparation takes about 10 minutes

VARIATION: For a special treat use canned salmon in place of the tuna.

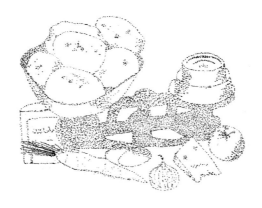

POTATOES WITH MONKFISH CREOLE

A lightly spiced fish topping.

SERVES 4

4 large baking potatoes
2 tbsps sunflower oil
1 onion, chopped
1 clove garlic, crushed
1 red chilli, seeded and chopped
½ green pepper, seeded and chopped
400g/14oz can chopped tomatoes
1 bay leaf
½ tsp mixed herbs
340g/12oz monkfish fillets, cut into cubes
175g/6oz cooked and peeled prawns
Knob of butter
Salt and pepper
Dash of Tabasco
Whole prawns to garnish

1. Cook the potatoes as directed (see Introduction).

2. Heat the oil in a saucepan and fry the onion and garlic until beginning to soften.

3. Add the chilli and green pepper and continue to fry for 3 minutes. Stir in the tomatoes, bay leaf and herbs and simmer for 5 minutes.

4. Add the fish and cook gently for 10 minutes. Stir in the prawns and continue to cook for a further 5 minutes.

5. When the potatoes are cooked, cut a deep cross in each one and scoop out the flesh. Mash well with a little butter, seasoning and a dash of Tabasco. Pile back into the skins.

6. Spoon the fish mixture onto the potatoes. Serve garnished with whole prawns.

TIME: Preparation takes about 10 minutes Cooking takes approximately 25 minutes.

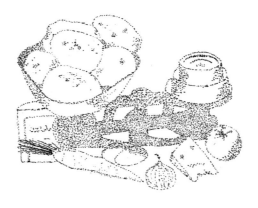

SEAFOOD AND TOMATO TOPPING

*Look out for packets of mixed seafood on the fresh fish counter or
in the freezer cabinet of your supermarket.*

SERVES 4

4 large baking potatoes
2 tbsps sunflower oil
1 clove garlic, crushed
340g/12oz tomatoes, skinned and chopped
5 tbsps white wine
460g/1lb mixed seafood, eg squid, mussels,
    prawns, scallops etc
1 tbsp chopped fresh parsley
Cornflour (if required)

1. Cook the potatoes as directed (see Introduction).

2. Heat the oil in a saucepan and fry the garlic for 1 minute.

3. Add the tomatoes and sauté for 2 minutes, then stir in the wine and bring to the boil.

4. Reduce the heat and simmer for 30 minutes or until thickened slightly.

5. Stir in the seafood and simmer gently for 10 minutes or until piping hot. Stir in the parsley.

6. If the sauce is still very runny, thicken with a little cornflour, mixed to a paste with cold water.

7. When the potatoes are cooked, cut in half and mash the flesh slightly if liked. Spoon the seafood mixture on top and serve immediately.

TIME: Preparation takes about 10 minutes Cooking takes approximately 40 minutes.

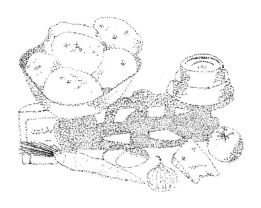

TUNA WITH MULTI-COLOURED PEPPERS

The ginger in this recipe gives it a slightly exotic flavour.

SERVES 4

4 large baking potatoes
2 tbsps olive oil
½ green pepper, seeded and diced
½ red pepper, seeded and diced
½ yellow pepper, seeded and diced
½ tsp black or white pepper
2.5cm/1 inch piece root ginger, peeled and
   grated
½ tsp crushed dried chillies
Salt and pepper
200g/7oz can tuna chunks, drained
Grated zest of ½ lemon
1 tbsp lemon juice
60g/2oz Cheddar cheese, grated

1. Cook the potatoes as directed (see Introduction).

2. Heat the oil in a frying pan and toss the peppers in the oil. Cook over a moderate heat for 5 minutes, stirring regularly until soft and beginning to brown slightly.

3. Add the ginger and crushed chillies, and season with salt and pepper.

4. Add the tuna, lemon zest and juice to the pan. Cook over a low heat for 2-3 minutes or until the tuna is hot.

5. When the potatoes are cooked, cut in half and scoop the flesh into a bowl. Mash well.

6. Add the tuna mixture to the potato and mix well.

7. Pile back into the potato skins and sprinkle with grated cheese. Return to the oven for 10 minutes or until the cheese melts.

TIME: Preparation takes about 10 minutes. Cooking takes approximately 15 minutes plus reheating.

VARIATION: Use canned salmon in place of the tuna.

MICROWAVE NOTES: If cooking the potatoes in a microwave, reheat for 2-3 minutes on 100% (high).

SMOKED HADDOCK AND TOMATO FILLED JACKETS

Smoked fish gives a lovely flavour to potatoes.

SERVES 4

---

4 large baking potatoes
225g/8oz smoked haddock, skinned
4 tbsps milk
Knob of butter
Pinch of grated nutmeg
Salt and pepper
1 beef tomato, chopped
1 tsp chopped fresh parsley
Fresh parsley, to garnish

---

1. Bake the potatoes as directed (see Introduction).

2. Put the haddock in an ovenproof dish. Pour over the milk and add the butter. Season with salt and pepper. Cover with foil.

3. About 20 minutes before the end of the potatoes' cooking time, place the fish on a lower shelf in the oven. Cook until it flakes easily with a fork.

4. Cut a lid off the cooked potatoes and discard. Scoop out the flesh and place in a large bowl. Carefully add the liquid from the fish and the nutmeg, and season to taste. Mash well.

5. Beat the tomato pieces into the potato along with the chopped parsley.

6. Pile the potato flesh back into the skins.

7. Pile the flaked fish on top of the potato and serve garnished with fresh parsley.

TIME: Preparation takes about 10 minutes, cooking takes approximately 20 minutes.

VARIATION: Use another smoked fish in this recipe, such as kipper, smoked mackerel or smoked cod.

COOKS TIP: Cooking the fish in the oven at the same time as the potatoes is a good way of saving fuel.

MICROWAVE NOTES: This recipe is not suitable for cooking in a microwave.

PRAWN AND AVOCADO FILLING

You can use smaller potatoes and serve this dish as a starter.

SERVES 4

4 large baking potatoes
1 ripe avocado, peeled and cubed
Grated zest and juice of ½ lime
120g/4oz cooked and peeled prawns
1 tomato, skinned and chopped
4 tbsps Greek yogurt
1 tbsp tomato purée
Dash of Tabasco
Salt and pepper
Ground paprika
Whole prawns to garnish (optional)

1. Cook the potatoes as directed (see Introduction).

2. Toss the avocado pieces in the lime juice to prevent discoloration.

3. Add the prawns and tomato and stir to combine.

4. In a small mixing bowl, mix together the yogurt, tomato purée, Tabasco, seasoning and lime zest.

5. Pour over the prawns and toss until well coated.

6. When the potatoes are cooked, cut a cross in the top of each one. Using a tea-towel, gently squeeze each potato to open out the cross slightly.

7. Pile the prawns on top and garnish with a sprinkling of paprika and a whole prawn if liked.

TIME: Preparation takes about 15 minutes.

WATCHPOINT: Avocados are ripe when they yield slightly upon being gently squeezed. If very soft, they will be mushy and will not have a good flavour.

VEGETABLE CURRY

Curry served with jacket potatoes makes a superb winter dish which is both warming and filling.

SERVES 4

4 large baking potatoes
2 tbsps ghee or sunflower oil
1 onion, chopped
2 cloves garlic, crushed
2 tsps ground coriander
1 tsp ground cumin
½ tsp ground fenugreek
½ tsp ground turmeric
½ tsp chilli powder
175g/6oz small cauliflower florets
2 carrots, sliced
1 red pepper, seeded and cut into small chunks
1 green pepper, seeded and cut into small chunks
120g/4oz mushrooms, halved or quartered
120g/4oz green beans cut into short lengths
½ pint vegetable stock
1 tsp cornflour (optional)
4 tbsps natural yogurt
3 tbsps crème fraîche

1. Cook the potatoes as directed (see introduction).

2. Melt the ghee or heat the oil in a large saucepan and fry the onion for about 5 minutes or until softened.

3. Stir in the garlic and spices and cook over a low heat for 3 minutes, stirring constantly to prevent the spices from burning.

4. Add the vegetables and toss over the heat for 3-4 minutes.

5. Pour in the stock and bring to the boil. Reduce the heat, cover and simmer for 30 minutes, stirring occasionally, until the vegetables are tender.

6. Thicken the liquid with a little cornflour mixed to a paste with cold water if liked. Stir in the yogurt and crème fraîche and heat gently.

7. When the potatoes are cooked, cut in half and mash the flesh if liked. Spoon over the curry and serve immediately.

TIME: Preparation takes about 15 minutes. Cooking time approximately 45 minutes.

SPICY GUACAMOLE POTATOES

Add a touch of spice to your potatoes with this Mexican dish.

SERVES 4

4 large baking potatoes
1 red or green chilli
½ small onion, cut into chunks
1 clove garlic, crushed
2 tomatoes, skinned, seeded and roughly
　chopped
¼ tsp ground cumin
¼ tsp ground coriander
1 large or 2 small ripe avocados
1 tbsp chopped coriander
1 tbsp chopped parsley
2 tsps lemon juice
Pinch of sugar
Salt and pepper
Tomato relish and fresh soured cream, to
　serve

1. Cook the potatoes as directed (see Introduction).

2. Cut the chilli in half and remove the seeds if liked. The seeds have the spicy heat of the chilli and the end dish will be 'hotter' if they are left in. Cut into chunks.

3. Put the onion, chilli and garlic in a food processor and process briefly to chop roughly.

4. Add the chopped tomato to the mixture in the food processor along with the cumin and ground coriander.

5. Cut the avocado in half lengthwise. Twist the halves genty in opposite directions to separate. Remove the stone and scoop out the flesh, scraping the skin well.

6. Add the avocado to the mixture in the food processor with the chopped coriander, parsley, lemon juice, sugar and seasoning. Process until the mixture is well combined and a fine, smooth consistency.

7. Chill until required.

8. When the potatoes are cooked, cut a cross in the top of each one. Using a tea-towel, gently squeeze each potato to open out the cross slightly.

9. Spoon the guacamole into the potatoes and top with tomato relish and soured cream.

TIME: Preparation takes about 15 minutes.

COLESLAW WITH BAVARIAN CHEESE

Smoked cheese added to coleslaw gives it an interesting and unusual flavour.

SERVES 4

4 large baking potatoes
½ small head of white cabbage, thinly
   shredded
2 carrots, grated
½ green pepper, seeded and thinly sliced
90g/3oz Bavarian smoked cheese
4 tbsps mayonnaise
4 tbsps fresh soured cream
Salt and Pepper
2 tbsps cashew nuts, toasted

1. Cook the potatoes as directed (see Introduction).

2. Put the shredded cabbage in a large mixing bowl and add the grated carrot and sliced pepper. Add the cheese

3. Mix together the mayonnaise and cream, and season well. Pour over the cabbage and toss until all the vegetables are coated.

4. When the potatoes are cooked, cut in half and mash the flesh if liked. Serve with the coleslaw piled on top. Sprinkle with toasted cashew nuts.

TIME: Preparation takes about 15 minutes.

VARIATION: Look out for smoked cheese with ham (for non vegetarians) or mushrooms. Both work well in this dish.

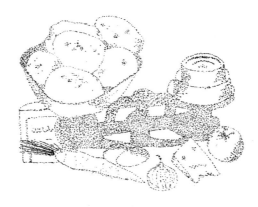

BLUE CHEESE AND WALNUT TOPPING

*This is a lovely filling for summer jacket potatoes as it has
a fresh and crunchy flavour.*

SERVES 4

4 large baking potatoes
1 apple, sliced
Lemon juice
4 sticks celery, sliced
60g/2oz walnuts, chopped
150g/5oz tub Greek yogurt
60g/2oz blue cheese
Salt and pepper
Lemon twists, to garnish

1. Cook the potatoes as directed (see Introduction).

2. Toss the sliced apple in a little lemon juice to prevent discoloration.

3. Put the celery, apple and walnuts in bowl and add the yogurt.

4. Crumble the blue cheese into the bowl, then toss all the ingredients together until well combined.

5. When the potatoes are cooked, cut a cross in the top of each one. Using a tea-towel, gently squeeze each potato to open out the cross slightly.

6. Season the potatoes with salt and pepper, then spoon the blue cheese mixture on top.

TIME: Preparation takes about 10 minutes.

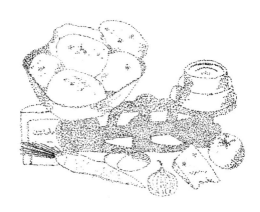

SPECIAL BAKED BEANS

*Much nicer than the canned variety, this recipe is based on
American Boston Baked Beans.*

SERVES 4

2 tbsps sunflower oil
1 piece belly pork, (optional)
1 clove garlic, crushed
1 large onion, chopped
400g/14oz can chopped tomatoes with
    herbs
60g/2oz molasses sugar
½ tsp ground cloves
1 tbsp whole grain mustard
2 x 432g/15½oz cans haricot or cannellini
    beans, drained and rinsed
4 large baking potatoes

1. Heat the oil in a frying pan and fry the belly of pork, if using, until browned on each side. Remove from the pan and place in an ovenproof dish.

2. Add the garlic and onion to the pan and sauté for 4 minutes or until soft. Stir in the tomatoes and bring to the boil.

3. Stir in the molasses sugar, cloves and mustard and stir until the sugar dissolves.

4. Add the beans to the pan and bring to the boil.

5. Pour the bean mixture into the ovenproof dish and cover.

6. Cook the potatoes as directed (see Introduction) with the beans alongside them.

7. When the potatoes are cooked, remove the pork from the beans and discard.

8. Cut the potatoes in half and serve topped with the beans.

TIME: Preparation takes about 15 minutes. Cooking takes approximately 1 hour 10 minutes.

COOK'S TIP: The pork is added to give flavour to the beans and is usually discarded after cooking. You can, however, omit the pork altogether or cut it into bite-size pieces and serve with the beans.

MICROWAVE NOTES: This recipe is not suitable for cooking in a microwave.

SPINACH AND CREAM CHEESE SOUFFLÉ BAKED POTATOES

These cheesy potatoes have a lighter texture than traditional baked potatoes.

SERVES 4

4 large baking potatoes
2 tbsps sunflower oil
1 small onion, finely chopped
175g/6oz fresh spinach, washed
120g/4oz cream cheese
Salt and pepper
3 eggs, separated
1 tbsp pine nuts

1. Cook the potatoes as directed (see Introduction).

2. Heat the oil in a saucepan and fry the onion until softened.

3. Add the spinach with just the water that clings to the leaves after washing and cook, covered, for about 5 minutes until wilted.

4. Drain off any water and roughly chop the spinach in a food processor.

5. Beat the spinach into the cream cheese. Season to taste.

6. When the potatoes are cooked, cut the tops off each one and scoop out the flesh. Mash well.

7. Beat the spinach mixture, egg yolks and pine nuts into the mashed potatoes.

8. Whisk the egg whites until standing in soft peaks, then carefully fold into the potato.

9. Spoon the mixture back into the potato skins.

10. Return to the oven and cook for 15-20 minutes or until risen and golden. Serve immediately.

TIME: Preparation takes about 10 minutes. Cooking takes approximately 25 minutes.

MICROWAVE NOTES: This recipe is not suitable for cooking in a microwave.

WELSH TATTIES

These potatoes are filled with leeks and a creamy cheese sauce.

SERVES 4

4 large baking potatoes
60g/2oz butter
460g/1lb leeks, thinly sliced
30g/1oz plain flour
280ml/½ pint milk
90g/3oz Caerphilly cheese, crumbled
Salt and pepper
Cherry tomatoes to garnish

1. Cook the potatoes as directed (see Introduction).

2. Melt the butter in a saucepan and fry the leeks over a low heat for 6-10 minutes or until soft.

3. Stir in the plain flour and cook for 1 minute.

4. Remove from the heat and gradually add the milk, stirring well after each addition.

5. Return the pan to the heat and cook over a low heat until thickened, stirring constantly.

6. Add the cheese to the sauce, and gently cook until most of the cheese melts.

7. When the potatoes are cooked, cut in half and scoop out the flesh. Mash well.

8. Add the leek mixture and beat until well combined. Season to taste. Spoon back into the potato skins and serve garnished with cherry tomatoes.

TIME: Preparation takes about 10 minutes. Cooking takes approximately 15 minutes.

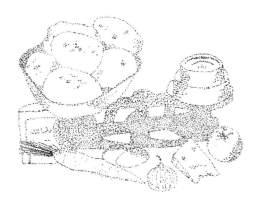

GARLICKY MUSHROOM TOPPING

Simple to prepare and quite irresistible.

SERVES 4

4 large baking potatoes
90g/3oz butter
1 small onion, finely chopped
3 cloves garlic, crushed
175g/6oz small button mushrooms,
    quartered
45g/1½oz toasted hazelnuts, chopped
Grated zest and juice of ½ lemon
Salt and pepper
2 tbsps chopped parsley

1. Cook the potatoes as directed (see Introduction).

2. Melt the butter in a frying pan and fry the onion until just softened.

3. Stir in the garlic and cook for 1 minute.

4. Add the mushrooms to the pan and fry for 4-5 minutes until softened.

5. Stir in the hazelnuts, lemon zest, juice, seasoning and parsley. Cook gently for 2 minutes.

6. When the potatoes are cooked, cut a wedge out of each one, and mash the flesh if liked. Spoon the mushroom mixture on top.

TIME: Preparation takes about 10 minutes. Cooking takes approximately 10 minutes.

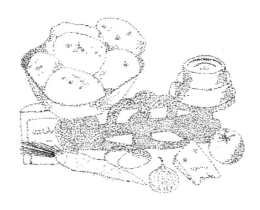

VEGETABLE CHILLI

Vegetarians need not miss out on this popular filling that goes so well with potatoes.

SERVES 4

4 large baking potatoes
2 tbsps sunflower oil
1 large onion, chopped
1 clove garlic, crushed
2 large carrots, diced
120g/4oz green beans, cut into 2.5cm/1–inch
  lengths
½ red pepper, seeded and cut into chunks
½ yellow pepper, seeded and cut into
  chunks
1 tsp crushed dried chillies
400g/14oz can chopped tomatoes
2 tbsps tomato purée
213g/7½oz can chickpeas, drained and
  rinsed
213g/7½oz can red kidney beans, drained
  and rinsed

1. Cook the potatoes as directed (see Introduction).

2. Heat the oil in a large saucepan and fry the onion and garlic gently for 5 minutes or until just softened.

3. Add the carrots, beans and pepper and toss over the heat for about 5 minutes until the vegetables begin to brown.

4. Stir in the crushed chillies and cook for 1 minute.

5. Stir in the tomatoes and tomato purée.

6. Mash half the chickpeas well with a fork, then add to the mixture along with the remaining chickpeas and the kidney beans. Stir well.

7. Bring gently to simmering point and simmer for 25-30 minutes.

8. When the potatoes are cooked, cut the tops off each one and scoop out the flesh. Mash well and pile back into the potato skins. Spoon the chilli mixture on top and serve.

TIME: Preparation takes about 20 minutes Cooking takes approximately 40 minutes.

73

MIXED BEAN SALAD

The beans turn simple jacket potatoes into a wholesome and filling meal.

SERVES 4

---

4 large baking potatoes
213g/7½oz can red kidney beans, drained and rinsed
225g/8oz can butter beans, drained and rinsed
½ x 432g/16oz can aduki beans, drained and rinsed
½ x 397g/14oz can cut green beans, drained and rinsed
60g/2oz sweetcorn kernels, defrosted
2 sticks celery, sliced
1 clove garlic
½ tsp salt
1 tsp mustard powder
1 tbsp cider vinegar
Freshly ground black pepper
6 tbsps olive oil
1 tsp snipped fresh chives
1 tsp chopped fresh tarragon
1 tsp chopped fresh parsley
Knob of butter
Black pepper

1. Cook the potatoes as directed (see Introduction).

2. Put the beans in a bowl and toss to mix. Stir in the sweetcorn and celery.

3. Using a pestle and mortar, pound the garlic and salt to a paste. Add the mustard powder, vinegar and pepper and mix thoroughly. Gradually blend in the olive oil.

4. Transfer the garlic mixture to a small cup and add the herbs, whisking with a fork until well blended.

5. Pour over the beans and toss until all the beans are well coated in the dressing.

6. When the potatoes are cooked, cut the tops off each one and scoop out the flesh.

7. Add a knob of butter and sprinkle with a little black pepper. Mash well. Pile back into the potato skins and serve with the bean salad.

TIME: Preparation takes about 10 minutes.

BAKED POTATOES WITH ORIENTAL-STYLE VEGETABLES

Brighten up jacket potatoes with a touch of the Orient.

SERVES 4

4 large baking potatoes
2 tbsps sunflower oil
1 clove garlic, crushed
2.5cm/1 inch piece root ginger, grated
120g/4oz baby corn
1 small red pepper, seeded and sliced
90g/3oz mange-tout, trimmed
8 spring onions, sliced
60g/2oz bean sprouts
6 tbsps oyster sauce
Salt and pepper
Knob of butter
2 tbsps chopped fresh coriander

1. Cook the potatoes as directed (see Introduction).

2. Heat the oil in a large frying pan or wok and add the garlic, ginger and baby corn. Stir fry for 2 minutes.

3. Add the pepper and mange-tout and stir fry for 2 minutes.

4. Add the spring onions and bean-sprouts. Stir fry for another 2 minutes or until all the vegetables are just tender.

5. Add the oyster sauce and cook for 1 minute, stirring constantly.

6. When the potatoes are cooked, cut in half and scoop out the flesh. Season with salt and pepper and add a knob of butter and the chopped coriander. Mash well.

7. Pile back into the skin of one half of each potato. Discard the remaining skins. Serve the potatoes with the vegetables.

TIME: Preparation takes about 10 minutes. Cooking takes approximately 7 minutes.

COOK'S TIP: Use the spare potato skins to make crispy potato skins as a starter or snack the following day. Deep fry until golden and serve with a dip of your choice.

CURRIED POTATO AND EGG JACKETS

Hard-boiled eggs are tossed in a creamy, lightly-spiced sauce, then used to stuff the potato.

SERVES 4

4 large baking potatoes
4 hard-boiled eggs, roughly chopped
3 sticks celery, sliced
2 spring onions, sliced
1 small green pepper, seeded and chopped
1-2 tsps mild curry paste
2 tbsps single cream
3 tbsps mayonnaise
2 tsps mango chutney
Paprika

1. Cook the potatoes as directed (see Introduction).

2. Put the chopped egg, celery, spring onions and green pepper into a mixing bowl.

3. In a small bowl mix together the curry paste, cream, mayonnaise and chutney until well combined.

4. Pour over the chopped eggs and toss until well coated.

5. When the potatoes are cooked, cut a lid off each one and scoop out the flesh. Mash well.

6. Add the potato to the egg mixture and mix well. Pile back into the potato skins and return to the oven for 10 minutes to heat through. Sprinkle with paprika and serve immediately.

TIME: Preparation takes about 10 minutes. Cooking takes approximately 10 minutes.

MICROWAVE NOTES: If cooking the potatoes in a microwave, reheat for 2-3 minutes on 100% (high).

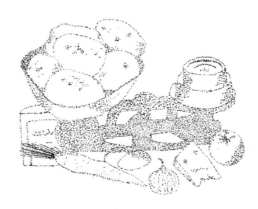

RATATOUILLE

Ratatouille is a Mediterranean dish which is ideal as a light meal when served on potatoes.

SERVES 4

---

4 large baking potatoes
2 tbsps olive oil
1 Spanish onion, sliced
1 clove garlic, crushed
½ small aubergine, chopped
½ red pepper, seeded and chopped
½ green pepper seeded and chopped
400g/14oz can chopped tomatoes
1 tbsp tomato purée
1 tsp chopped fresh oregano
Few fresh basil leaves, torn into pieces
5 tbsps red wine or vegetable stock
Salt and pepper

---

1. Cook the potatoes as directed (see Introduction).

2. Heat the oil in a large frying pan and sauté the onion until beginning to soften. Add the garlic and cook for 1 minute.

3. Stir in the aubergine and peppers and fry over a medium heat until just beginning to soften.

4. Add the tomatoes, tomato purée, oregano, basil and wine or stock. Bring gently to the boil, then reduce the heat and simmer for 30 minutes or until the liquid has reduced slightly.

5. When the potatoes are cooked, cut in half and place on a serving plate.

6. Season the ratatouille to taste and spoon over the potatoes. Serve immediately.

TIME: Preparation takes about 20 minutes. Cooking takes approximately 25 minutes.

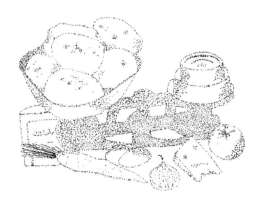

CAMEMBERT MELTS

A simple creamy cheese filling makes these potatoes a super light snack. They can also be served as an accompaniment to other dishes.

SERVES 4

4 large baking potatoes
225g/8oz Camembert cheese
225g/8oz cottage cheese
8 spring onions, sliced
Salt and pepper
Pinch of grated nutmeg

1. Cook the potatoes as directed (see Introduction).

2. Remove the rind from the Camembert and discard.

3. Mash the Camembert together with the cottage cheese, using a fork, until the cheeses are evenly combined.

4. Add the spring onions to the cheese, and season with salt, pepper and a little grated nutmeg.

5. When the potatoes are cooked, cut a lid off each one and set aside. Scoop out the flesh and beat into the cheese mixture, then pile back into the potato skins.

6. Replace the lids and return to the oven for 10-15 minutes until the cheese begins to melt.

TIME: Preparation takes about 10 minutes. Cooking takes approximately 15 minutes.

VARIATION: Use another soft cheese such as Brie in place of the Camembert.

COOK'S TIP: Allow the Camembert or Brie to stand at room temperature for about an hour before use so that it will soften and be easier to mash. If you have difficulty mashing the cheese, cut into small cubes instead.

MICROWAVE NOTES: If cooking the potatoes in a microwave, reheat for 2-3 minutes on 100% (high) or until the cheese begins to melt.

CHEESY HERB POTATOES

Plain baked potatoes are transformed by the inclusion of herbs. Serve as a light meal or as an accompaniment to other dishes.

SERVES 2

2 large baking potatoes
1 small onion, finely chopped
30g/1oz butter
1 tbsp chopped fresh rosemary
1 tbsp chopped fresh thyme
1 tbsp chopped fresh sage
Salt and pepper
2 tbsps cream cheese
30g/1oz red Leicester, grated
30g/1oz Cheddar cheese, grated
Chopped parsley, to garnish

1. Cook the potatoes as directed (see Introduction).

2. Just before the potatoes are cooked, put the onion and butter in a frying pan and cook gently for about 5 minutes or until the onion is soft but not browned.

3. Add the rosemary, thyme, sage and seasoning and toss together until well combined.

4. Cut the cooked potatoes in half and scoop out the flesh. Mash well. Beat in the cream cheese.

5. Add the potato mixture to the pan and cook over a low heat until piping hot.

6. Pile back into the potato skins and mark with a fork.

7. Scatter two halves with the red Leicester and the other halves with the Cheddar cheese. Return to the oven for a few minutes until the cheese is melted, or brown under a preheated grill. Garnish with chopped parsley and serve.

TIME: Preparation takes about 5 minutes. Cooking takes approximately 10 minutes.

SOUFFLÉ POTATOES WITH CARROT AND ASPARAGUS

A special light meal with an unusual combination of vegetables.

SERVES 2

---

2 large baking potatoes
175g/6oz carrots, sliced
½ small onion, chopped
15g/½oz butter
2 tsps plain flour
6 tbsps milk
2 eggs, separated
Salt and pepper
Pinch of grated nutmeg
½ bunch asparagus
½ orange

---

1. Cook the potatoes in a conventional oven as directed (see Introduction).

2. Bring a small saucepan of water to the boil and add the carrots and onion. Cook for 10 minutes or until the carrots are tender.

3. Drain and place in a food processor.

4. Melt the butter in a saucepan. Stir in the flour and cook over a low heat for 1 minute.

5. Remove from the heat and gradually add the milk, stirring well after each addition.

6. Return the pan to the heat and cook over a low heat until thickened, stirring constantly.

7. Pour over the carrots in the food processor and process until smooth.

8. Beat in the egg yolks, and season with salt, pepper and nutmeg.

9. When the potatoes are cooked, cut the tops off each one and scoop out the flesh. Mash well. Beat into the carrot mixture.

10. Whisk the egg whites until standing in soft peaks, then carefully fold into the carrot mixture.

11. Pile back into the potato skins and return to the oven for 15-20 minutes until risen and golden.

12. Meanwhile, cook the asparagus in boiling water for 5-8 minutes until just tender. Grate the zest from the orange and squeeze a little juice.

13. Serve the asparagus with the potatoes. Sprinkle the asparagus with orange juice, zest and a little nutmeg.

TIME: Preparation takes about 15 minutes. Cooking takes approximately 40 minutes.

MICROWAVE NOTES: This recipe is not suitable for cooking in a microwave.

EGGS FLORENTINE IN A JACKET

A combination of classic and everyday.

SERVES 2

2 large baking potatoes
90g/3oz chopped spinach, frozen
30g/1oz butter
Salt and pepper
Pinch of grated nutmeg
2 eggs
1 tbsp cornflour
120ml/4 fl oz milk
2 tbsps grated Parmesan cheese

1. Cook the potatoes in a conventional oven as directed (see Introduction).

2. Put the spinach in a small saucepan and heat gently over a very low heat until it begins to defrost.

3. Add the butter and cook for 3 minutes. Season well with salt, pepper and nutmeg.

4. Lightly poach the eggs in gently simmering water or use an egg poacher until just set. When cooked, place in cold water until required.

5. Put the cornflour in a saucepan with a little of the milk. Mix to a smooth paste.

6. Stir in the remaining milk, then cook over a low heat, stirring constantly until the sauce thickens. Season well. Stir in half of the Parmesan cheese.

7. When the potatoes are cooked, cut the tops off each one and scoop out the flesh. Mash well.

8. Pile back into the potato skins and pack down well, forming small hollows.

9. Spoon the spinach mixture into the two potatoes. Remove the eggs from the water and drain well. Place on top of the spinach.

10. Spoon over the sauce and sprinkle with the remaining cheese.

11. Return to the oven for 15 minutes to heat through.

TIME: Preparation takes about 5 minutes. Cooking takes approximately 25 minutes.

MICROWAVE NOTES: This recipe is not suitable for cooking in a microwave.

KIPPER AND EGG MASH

This first-rate fish dish is ideal for brunch.

SERVES 2

---

2 large baking potatoes
225g/8oz pkt frozen boil-in-the-bag kippers
1 hard-boiled egg, roughly chopped
2 tbsps frozen peas, defrosted
Salt and pepper
1 tbsp grated red Leicester cheese
1 tbsp grated Cheddar cheese
Hard-boiled egg slices and sprigs of dill, to
garnish

---

1. Cook the potatoes as directed (see Introduction).

2. Cook the kippers according to the pack instructions.

3. Put the chopped egg in a mixing bowl with the peas. When the fish is cooked, cut the package and pour the juices over the egg and peas.

4. Flake the fish and add to the bowl.

5. When the potatoes are cooked, cut in half and scoop out the flesh. Mash well and add to the fish.

6. Beat the fish and potato together until well combined. Taste and season as desired.

7. Pile back into the potato skins. Mix together the two cheeses and sprinkle on top. Return to the oven for 10-15 minutes to heat through and brown the cheese.

8. Serve garnished with egg slices and sprigs of dill.

TIME: Preparation takes about 5 minutes. Cooking takes approximately 30 minutes.

MICROWAVE NOTES: If cooking the potatoes in a microwave, reheat for 1½ minutes on 100% (high).

91

SARDINE AND TOMATO HASH

You only need a few fresh ingredients to make this simple stand-by meal.

SERVES 2

2 large baking potatoes
1 tbsp olive oil
4 large spring onions, sliced
1 clove garlic, crushed
1 stick celery, chopped
Few fresh basil leaves
120g/4oz can sardines in tomato sauce
Salt and pepper
Knob of butter
Dash of Worcestershire sauce

1. Cook the potatoes as directed (see Introduction).

2. Heat the oil in a small pan and fry the spring onions and garlic for 2-3 minutes or until the onions are softened.

3. Add the celery and cook for another 3-4 minutes.

4. Tear the basil into small pieces and add to the pan along with the sardines in their sauce. Mix well. Season and add the butter and Worcestershire sauce.

5. When the potatoes are cooked, scoop out the flesh, keeping as whole as possible, and roughly cut into cubes.

6. Add to the pan and toss over the heat for a few minutes before piling back into the potato skins. Serve immediately.

TIME: Preparation takes about 5 minutes. Cooking takes approximately 10 minutes.

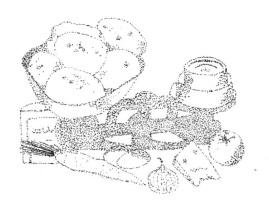

CRAB AND PRAWN FILLED SPUDS

A light and attractive seafood dish.

SERVES 2

---

2 large baking potatoes
170g/5½oz can crab meat, drained
60g/2oz cooked and peeled prawns
4 spring onions, sliced
60ml/4 tbsps mayonnaise
Grated zest and juice of ½ lime
Salt and pepper
Whole prawns to garnish (optional)

---

1. Cook the potatoes as directed (see Introduction).

2. Put the crab-meat in a bowl and stir in the prawns and sliced spring onions.

3. Mix together the mayonnaise, lime zest and juice. Pour over the crab and stir until well combined. Season to taste with salt and pepper.

4. When the potatoes are cooked, cut in half, scoop out the flesh and mash well.

5. Pile back into the potato skins and top with the crab mixture. Alternatively, mix together the crab mixture and potato before returning to the skins and heat through in the oven for 10-15 minutes.

6. Serve garnished with a whole prawn if liked.

TIME: Preparation takes about 5 minutes.

VARIATION: Use crab sticks if preferred.

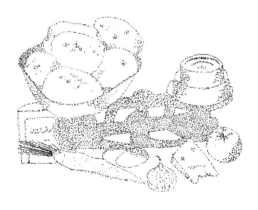

SMOKED SALMON AND CAVIAR

Don't be put off by the name of the dish; this simple lunch or supper dish really is affordable.

SERVES 2

2 large baking potatoes
90g/3oz smoked salmon pâté
2 tbsps crème fraîche or Greek yogurt
Salt and pepper
1 tbsp lemon juice
2 tsps chopped fresh dill
2 small sprigs fresh dill
2 tsps lumpfish caviar

1. Cook the potatoes as directed (see Introduction).

2. Cut the tops off the cooked potatoes, scoop the flesh into a bowl and mash well.

3. Beat the pâté in a medium sized bowl until softened slightly, then beat in the crème fraîche or yogurt.

4. Beat the pâté mixture into the potato flesh, then season to taste with salt and pepper.

5. Stir in the lemon juice and chopped dill.

6. Pile the mixture back into the potato skins, and return to the oven for 10-15 minutes to heat through. Serve topped with a sprig of dill and a little caviar.

TIME: Preparation takes about 10 minutes. Reheating takes approximately 10 minutes.

MICROWAVE NOTES: If cooking the potatoes in a microwave, reheat for 1½ minutes on 100% (high).

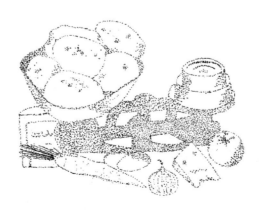

ITALIAN HAM AND CHEESE FILLING

A quick and easy filling with a decidedly Continental feel.

SERVES 1

---

1 large baking potato
30g/1oz fresh Parmesan cheese
15g/½oz butter
1 slice Parma ham, cut into thin strips
½ tsp horseradish sauce
2 tbsps fresh soured cream

---

1. Cook the potato as directed (see Introduction).

2. Using a potato peeler, thinly slice the Parmesan cheese into small flakes or grate the cheese.

3. When the potato is cooked, cut in half and scoop out the flesh. Mash well with the butter.

4. Reserve a little of the cheese, then beat into the potato along with the ham and horseradish sauce.

5. Pile the potato mixture back into the potato skins and return to the oven for 10 minutes to heat through.

6. Place on a serving dish and top with the soured cream and reserved cheese. Serve immediately.

TIME: Preparation takes about 5 minutes. Reheating takes approximately 10 minutes.

MICROWAVE NOTES: If cooking the potato in a microwave, reheat for 1 minute on 100% (high).

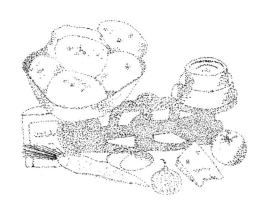

CRUNCHY CHICKEN AND SWEETCORN TOPPING

This supper dish for one is ideal for using up leftover chicken.

SERVES 1

1 large baking potato
120g/4oz cooked chicken, cut into bite-sized
    pieces
Small stick celery, thinly sliced or chopped
2 tbsps sweetcorn kernels, defrosted if
    frozen
2 tbsps crème fraîche or Greek yogurt
Salt and pepper
1 tsp chopped fresh mint or pinch of dried
    mint
Dash of Tabasco
Fresh mint, to garnish

1. Cook the potato as directed (see Introduction).

2. Put the chicken, celery and sweetcorn in a bowl.

3. Mix together the crème fraîche or yogurt, seasoning, mint and Tabasco, and pour over the chicken mixture, stirring until well coated.

4. When the potato is cooked, cut in half and mash the flesh slightly. Spoon the chicken mixture on top, garnish with fresh mint and serve immediately.

TIME: Preparation takes about 5 minutes.

VARIATION: Use ham if you do not have any leftover chicken. Cooked turkey can also be used, making this an ideal Boxing Day lunch.

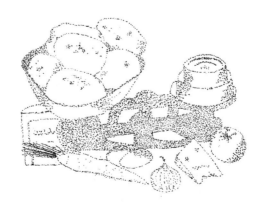

CRISPY CHEESE AND BACON JACKETS

A super supper dish, delicious served with home-made pickle.

SERVES 1

---

1 large baking potato
60g/2oz bacon, diced
½ onion, finely chopped
1 tbsp sunflower oil
Salt and pepper
30g/1oz Gruyère cheese, grated
1 tbsp fresh breadcrumbs

---

1. Cook the potato as directed (see Introduction).

2. Mix together the bacon and onion.

3. Heat the oil in a frying pan and fry the bacon and onion gently for 5 minutes.

4. Drain off any liquid, then increase the heat and cook for about 5 minutes or until the bacon and onion begin to crisp.

5. Cut the cooked potato in half and scoop out the flesh into a bowl. Mash well.

6. Beat the bacon and onion into the potato and season to taste with salt and pepper. Mix in half the cheese, then pile back into the potato skins.

7. Mix the remaining cheese with the breadcrumbs and sprinkle over the potatoes.

8. Place under a preheated grill and cook until golden.

TIME: Preparation takes about 10 minutes. Cooking takes approximately 12 minutes.

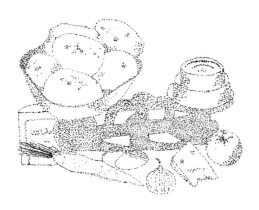

BLT JACKETS

This popular sandwich filling goes just as well with jacket potatoes.

SERVES 2

2 large baking potatoes
1 tbsp olive oil
4 spring onions, sliced
1 clove garlic, crushed
200g/7oz can tomatoes
1 tsp mixed herbs
2 rashers back bacon or 4 rashers streaky
  bacon
Few crisp lettuce leaves
2 tbsps mayonnaise (optional)

1. Cook the potatoes as directed (see Introduction).

2. Heat the oil in a small saucepan and sauté the spring onions and garlic for 1 minute or until just beginning to soften,

3. Stir in the tomatoes and herbs. Bring to the boil, then reduce the heat and simmer gently for 5 minutes, breaking up the tomatoes with the back of a spoon as they cook.

4. Cook the bacon in the oven alongside the potatoes for 15 minutes or under a preheated grill until crisp and golden.

5. When the potatoes are cooked, cut in half and mash the flesh if liked.

6. Arrange a few lettuce leaves on top of the potatoes and spoon on the tomato sauce. Top with the bacon and mayonnaise if liked. Serve immediately.

TIME: Preparation takes about 5 minutes. Cooking takes approximately 15 minutes.

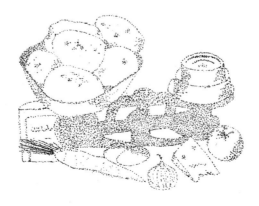

SCRAMBLED EGGS AND SMOKED SALMON

An ideal special supper or brunch for two.

SERVES 2

2 large baking potatoes
2 eggs
2 tbsps milk
Salt and pepper
Pinch of grated nutmeg
Pinch of cayenne pepper
45g/1½oz butter
60g/2oz smoked salmon, cut into strips
1 tsp snipped chives
Grilled tomatoes and fresh chives to serve

1. Cook the potatoes as directed (see Introduction).

2. Put the eggs in a small bowl with the milk, seasoning, nutmeg and cayenne and beat with a fork until frothy.

3. When the potatoes are cooked, cut in half and dot with a little of the butter. Mash the flesh slightly and keep warm.

4. Melt the remaining butter in a small saucepan and pour in the egg mixture. Cook over a low heat, stirring constantly, to scramble the egg as it cooks.

5. When almost set, stir in the smoked salmon and chives, cook for a few seconds longer, then pile onto the potatoes.

6. Serve with grilled tomatoes and garnish with fresh chives.

TIME: Preparation takes about 2 minutes. Cooking takes approximately 4 minutes.

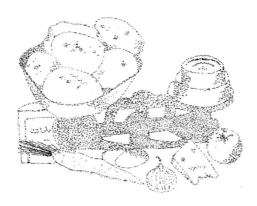

BANGERS 'N' BEANS

*An all-time favourite with the kids, which is made more nutritious
by adding a little cheese.*

SERVES 2

2 medium baking potatoes
4 pork chipolatas
225g/8oz can reduced sugar and salt baked
   beans
60g/2oz Gruyere or Cheddar cheese, cubed
Dash of Worcestershire sauce
Knob of butter
2 tbsps milk

1. Cook the potatoes as directed (see Introduction).

2. Cook the chipolatas under a preheated grill for 8-10 minutes until cooked through and golden. Cut the sausages on the diagonal, into 2.5cm/1-inch slices.

3. When the potatoes are almost cooked, gently heat the baked beans in a small saucepan. When hot, stir in the sausages, cheese and Worcestershire sauce.

5. Cut a lid off each potato and set aside. Scoop out the flesh, and spoon into a bowl. Add the butter and milk, and mash well.

6. Pile the potato back into the skins, spoon the bean mixture on top and serve.

TIME: Preparation takes about 2 minutes. Cooking takes approximately 12 minutes.

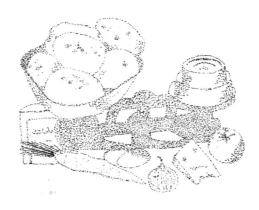

SLIMMER'S DELIGHT

*Make sure you do not add any extra peanut butter and this will be a
healthy and low calorie meal.*

SERVES 1

1 medium baking potato
120g/4oz cottage cheese
30g/1oz mandarin segments in natural juice,
    drained weight
1 tbsp sunflower seeds
Salt and pepper
2 tsps peanut butter

1. Cook the potato as directed (see
Introduction).

2. Put the cottage cheese in a bowl and stir
in the mandarin segments and sunflower
seeds.

3. When the potato is cooked, cut off the
top and carefully scoop out most of the
flesh. Put in a mixing bowl and season
lightly.

4. Add the peanut butter and mash well.

5. Return the potato to the skin and return
to the oven for 5-10 minutes to heat
through.

6. Pile the cottage cheese mixture on top
and serve with a crisp green salad.

TIME: Preparation takes about 5 minutes. Reheating takes approximately 10 minutes.

MICROWAVE NOTES: If cooking the potato in a microwave, reheat for
1 minute on 100% (high).

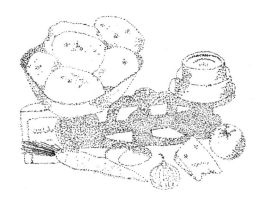

Index